SCARS she can't hide

Dings R Veds

"The pillow's secret: you are not alone."

BlueRose ONE.com
Stories Matter
New Delhi • London

BLUEROSE PUBLISHERS
India | U.K.

For permissions requests or inquiries regarding this publication, please contact:

BLUEROSE PUBLISHERS
www.BlueRoseONE.com
info@bluerosepublishers.com
+91 8882 898 898
+4407342408967

ISBN: 978-93-7018-328-5

Cover Design: Aman Sharma
Typesetting: Pooja Sharma

First Edition: March 2025

Thank You to Myself,

For staying with the wrong people, Learning hard lessons.

For leaving the right ones, Teaching them lessons too. In the end, We all grew.

Introduction ♡

Once upon a time, I hated books. Seriously, I couldn't stand them. Reading was something other people did – people who had way more patience than me. But then, something unexpected happened. My tuition sister, Jayashree, somehow tricked me into picking up a book. I'm still not sure how she did it – maybe it was a miracle, or maybe it was just a big mistake – but here I am now, standing with a huge collection of books. Who would've thought?

Now, here's the funny part. The things I swore I'd never do? The stuff I thought I'd never be caught dead doing? Yeah, I ended up doing all of it. Life is weird like that. And all those things I avoided ended up pushing me into situations I never imagined.

I discovered my talent for writing during one of the hardest times in my life. I was going through a tough situation, one that felt like it had no cure, no therapy, and no people left to help. I was alone in a dark room with just my notebook and a pen. In that lonely place, I started scribbling my thoughts, and that's when my brother Arulmurugan noticed my writing. That's how my journey began.

At 15, I had this big dream of writing a book and becoming an author. So, I wrote my first motivational book. But then I thought, Who am I, a novice, to go and give others advice on motivation? I wasn't even fully motivated myself! So, I scrapped that idea. But after some time, I tried again with another motivational book. It was better than the first one, but still, something didn't feel right, so I dropped that too.

Finally, I had a lightbulb moment. I decided to write about the struggles of teenage girls in India – something I knew from my own experience. I poured my heart into it, writing slowly and steadily. Then, out of nowhere, I heard a real breakup story that shook me. I couldn't handle how much it hurt me to hear it, so I wrote a poem called The Breakup. And I thought, Is this really me? Am I actually good at this?

From that moment, I became a sponge for stories – my own and others'. This book is the result of that journey, filled with my feelings and the stories of the people I've met. It's funny how life can turn you into something you never thought you'd be, isn't it?

Note from the Author

This book is for the overthinkers, the ones who feel lost and betrayed by those they loved the most. It's for the girls searching for peace in a world that only seems to judge, for those craving love but finding themselves trapped in the shadow of others' expectations.

It's written from the raw, unfiltered perspective of

a teenage girl—a voice that often goes unheard. It captures the pain of soft hearts hardened by the world, shaped by experiences that stole innocence and replaced it with resilience.

This is her story, her struggle, and her transformation. How the wounds of betrayal turned her gentle soul into a weapon—a sharp pistol. And when she finally fought back, the same people who hurt her asked, "Why did she do this to me?"

This book isn't just a story; it's a mirror reflecting the silent screams and untold stories of every girl who's been misunderstood, judged, and left to find her own strength in a world that broke her.

You are not alone, and these pages are for you.

Special thanks to

Ramasamy(daddy)

Gomathi(mummy)

Riduvarshini (sista)

Kaviya (sis)

Venktesh (bro)

Break Up

Break up;

It kills, it's a drug

I had a beautiful butterfly dancing in my stomach.

It's a sign that you entered into a fantasy world.

You blindly believe their word and fall easily with them,

They make you feel special,

They make you feel you are a rare gem… Having a call convo never ends before 4hrs, Having a new feel with a special memory, Still, you are in their fantasy world.

Finally, you're addicted;

It's a loop to your drug. Butterflies are faded; Promise are broken.

Care replaced as restriction; Fantasy replaced to hell.

All misunderstanding start; Not ready to listen.

Silence kills; Action scratches. Where all the shit,

Fucking feelings gone?

Again, I was in the bed with the same hell, with extra offers.

All night cried in silence, Only me;

My bed; My pillow;

My bedsheet;

And the dark room to escape reality. Survived with the moonlight;

Where my life swings in the dark fight. He changed;

He moved on.

But still I'm fighting to find where all the butterflies have gone.

Faded; Drowned.

He played game; I played a role not in his soul.

Finally…he changed, I'm still fighting with myself

to come out,

How…?

-Dings R Veds

Contents

1. How God Tests Us...

When it's time for idle talk,
Many gather, filling the room,
But when help is needed,
Half the names from your contacts vanish,
Lost like whispers in the wind.

Fingers enough to count,
The true ones who remain,
Among them, a few with hearts pure,
But situations keep them away,
Even though they wish to stay.

And then there are those,
Whose hearts are only open
When it's convenient,
They vanish when asked to give,
Leaving you to wonder, is this life?

A test of bonds, a measure of love,
A fleeting glimpse of what truly is

This, indeed, is life's eternal test.

Dings R Veds...

2. She Carries the Wound

She carries the wound, untended, unhealed,
A silent scar, her pain concealed.
But instead of a fight with the past,
She lets it rest, her strength amassed.

No longer bound by the old despair,
She faces herself, her soul laid bare.
In the quiet of her inner fight,
She strives to mend, to find the light.

The wound remains, a silent peal,
Yet she competes, to set it free.
In healing's race, she takes her stand,
With tender strength, she holds her hand.

Dings R Veds...

3. She Knows Everything

She knows, she knows everything
She knows how much I cried for him…
How much pain I endured for him…
She knows I placed my life in him…

Even after knowing this, she betrayed me,
She took him away from me…
But even if she takes him,
He would come back saying,
"No matter what, I loved you truly."

But he didn't do that either…
He left too…

So now, let them both go,
Let them leave…
It's unbearable…
The pain of being cheated by someone so close,
A soulmate, is overwhelming…

But, thankfully,

God showed me their true faces early…

In the process of healing,

I found so many people,

I connected with them…

If those two were my world,

These others are the ones

Who have shown me there's much more to see…

So, it's all for the better…

Dings R Veds...

4. Days Pass

Days will pass, and time may heal,
But the heart's wounds are slow to seal.
They linger on, though hard we try,
To find the pieces pain left behind.

The pieces fall, the hurt remains,
Until the heart turns into grains.
Yet I will fight, I won't give in,
Until the dust fades from within.

Dings R Veds...

5. The Rising Phoenix

When nothing goes as planned,
Am I the wrong girl?
Maybe to you, yes.
But to me, I am right.

Shut off your endless noise,
Your chaos no longer consumes me.
I want to open a new window,
A place where all your lies,
Your games,
Can finally drift away.

I've been innocent—
Too innocent—
Until you tore open my defenses.
I kept her hidden,
That girl inside me.
The child, fragile yet strong,
The one who refused to break.

But you forced her out.
You opened her cage,
Unleashed the fire she held back for so long.
And now, here I stand.

No longer caged,
No longer silenced.
This is me—
The real me,
Unafraid and unbroken.

Thank you—
Not for your cruelty,
But for waking me up,
For showing me I never needed you.
Now, I step forward,
Free from your chains,
Ready to claim my peace,
My identity,
And my life.

Dings R Veds...

6. The Innocent Prisoner

No more ways to prove myself,
No more energy left to speak.
In everyone's life, I feel like a prisoner,
Caged in a role I never wanted to play.
They see me as the villain,
But I never asked for this script.

The ones I held closest didn't understand.
They believed my opponent's lies,
Deceived by her clever façade.

She played her part so well—
And here I am,
A broken heart, overthinking
Again and again,
Unable to stop the cycle.

They abandoned the true soul,
Choosing to dance with the wrong people.
I try to make my heart strong,
But my innocence keeps it fragile.
They know I'm innocent—
Yet they take my peace,
Turn it into their twisted entertainment.

Don't tell me you've changed.
It's not change I see;
It's my pain mirrored back at you,
A reflection of your guilt.
This is me—pure, raw, real.

If you accept me, stay.
If not, walk away.
No one is begging you to stay,
And I won't lose myself to keep you.

Self-respect is no longer negotiable.
Why should I feel sorrow
For the one who lost the diamond?
You call me a playgirl?
Fine, you're right.
But not in the way you think.
I am a playgirl,
Playing with my own feelings
Day and night,
Trying to escape a world
That destroys my peace,
A world that steals my identity.

Dings R Veds...

7. The Door Have Closed

I've finally uncovered the truth that kept me stuck for so long.
It's nothing but an addiction that fueled my dopamine,
An attachment woven with oxytocin.

Yes, it hurts deeply every time I close my eyes
And sink into the sea of memories.
If it didn't hurt, it would mean I had betrayed our love.
The pain, the anguish—they tear at my soul,
Disrupt my mental peace, steal my happiness.

If I felt nothing, then I wouldn't be the one
Who truly loved you with all my heart.
But I'm in a process now—one of healing, of transformation.
So, stop knocking on the same door.

I'm shifting to a new space within myself,
A place of serenity and joy.
You might still hold the key,
But I've changed the lock,
And it will never fit again.

You played with my emotions,
Exploited my vulnerability—my greatest weakness.
But I've found strength in recognizing it,
And I've chosen to evolve.

So don't try again,
Because the last piece of what you took for granted is gone.
You'll never find the same version of me again.

Here's a word of advice:
Don't cheat—not just on me, but on anyone.
It doesn't destroy them; it destroys you.

Dings R Veds...

8. Lessons From Bonds

Some friends will show you what's truly kind,
While others are snakes, playing tricks with your mind.
Some bring you joy when you're feeling low,
While others leave scars as they choose to go.

Some teach you lessons, though their time is brief,
And some stay with love, bringing you relief.
But jealousy, ego—they creep in too,
From friends you thought were loyal and true.

Don't search for one who matches your soul,
It's a journey of pain that can take its toll.
Instead, find a group where you laugh and talk,
Where bonds are easy, and you let life walk.

This world is tricky, and snakes will appear,
Even after knowing them for years.
So, walk your path with your head held high,
Let people come and let them say goodbye.

Dings R Veds...

9. Fate's Design

No intent to hurt, no wish to stray,
Yet here I stand, torn away.
I love you still, but fate's cruel art
Draws its lines to keep us apart.

I never meant to cause you pain,
Yet my shadow brought only strain.
I dreamed to be your haven, your light,
But instead, I became your sorrowed night.

So long I searched, so long I yearned,
Only to watch as the tides have turned.
In a fleeting moment, love slipped away,
A treasure lost, though I begged it to stay.

Now, though distant, my heart remains,
Bound to you through joy and pain.
For even as fate tears us in two,
I will forever belong to you.

Dings R Veds...

10. Love's Second Chance

Nothing is lost,
But you and me in the shadows' embrace.
Let's dance once more, from start to end,
A rhythm of love that time cannot bend.

It's the beginning, just you and me,
Returning to one, where our love was free.
Where whispers of joy were the songs we'd sing,
And the world dissolved in the warmth we'd bring.

Let's relive the moments that brought us here,
The laughter, the whispers, the love so clear.
Rekindle the flame, let it burn anew,
A light in the darkness for me and you.

For nothing is lost in this timeless refrain,
Except you and me, in love, again.

Dings R Veds...

11. Scars of Love

You came into my life like a dream,
A spark of hope, a gentle gleam.
I gave my heart, I gave my all,
But you let me crash, let me fall.

You moved on, so quick, so free,
Left me alone with memories.
With her, my friend, you chose to be,
And yet your shadow won't leave me.

Each night I cry, the pain won't fade,
Your name echoes in the life we made.
You stole the love I gave so true,
And left my heart broken in two.

I try to move, but you're still there,
In every breath, in every stare.
Why did you come, just to leave?
A wound that time can't yet relieve.

Dings R Veds…

12. My Sunshine

"You are my sunshine, under the seashore,
My moonlight, to fly a blue kite,
To lose sight, in a new light.
You are my superstar, wrapping all my flash cards,
To make my bond board, just beneath the star.
You are my sunshine, under the seashore,
My super star, wrapping all my flash cards, once more"

Dings R Veds…

13. Ghost and Batman

Forever ♾ bond...!

"I wake up fresh every day,
Open your message, get blush in many ways.
I have a crush on you, but
Still, I didn't open up to you..
Looking at the moon, all stars got fade,

Just you and me,
Looking for shade,
So, we don't get tread.
Every night, a bright convo gleams,
Ending with sweet dreams, it seems
The bliss dream got theme,
So, I wake up with love of extreme..!

Dings R Veds…

14. Swap and Cheat

Yeah, you're playing with my feeling
And devasted to get off
To make my gut feeling strong
You changed…
For no reason...?
You Swapped me
To make you feel better...
You may be happy to trade me
But…
Again, you won't get me
As your first sight
Make your heart firm
So, you won't get cheated
By him again...

Dings R Veds…

15. The Dance of Opposites

People always love the moon
Because…
It gives light with calm and cool
People who are in dumb tune
They bear the bump moon
People always hate the sun
Because…
It gives light with hot and heat
People who are in dump tune
They hate the sun bloom

But they don't know that without the sun,
No moonlight would shine, having no fun.
They mix up things, separating them wide,
As moon and sun, yours and mine.
But it's not you and me,
It's we and us, unity.

Dings R Veds…

16. The Shit I fit

The world, I born was strict,
The world, I need was tricked,
I wrote a script; in my bucket list,
And I exist with fucking shit!

My guts whispered to commit,
So, I enlisted my grit!
To make sure nothing is unfit,
To build the world that fit my shit…!

Dings R Veds…

17. Let It Be

Let's go....!
The path was hidden,
Let's find....!
The maps are stolen,
Let's enquire....!
The groups are broken,
Let's re-join....!
The trust is faded,
Let it be....!

Dings R Veds…

18. Bond with the Moon

Just staring at the star,
Wishing you weren't so far.
Talking soft with the moon,
Hoping for a cuddle soon.

The night feels calm and still,
The moon knows how I feel.
It listens when I'm blue,
A bond so pure, so true.

No need for words to say,
The moon lights up my way.
In its glow, I find my tune,
Forever bound to the moon.

Dings R Veds…

19.Only You

Nothing lasts forever, this we know,
But you have yourself, and that will grow.
Dance with the river, go with the flow,
It's you and your glow that will always show.

Just you and your soul, let the rhythm align,
No need for another, your heart is divine.
Vibe with yourself, let your spirit shine,
You are enough, a star by design.

No one lives within, it's only you,
The love you give is pure and true.
In your own glow, find what's real,
Self-love's the bond no time can steal.

Dings R Veds…

20. The Overthinker's Plight

Overthinking steals the light,
Turns day to dark and wrong to right.
Small thoughts spiral, endless chain,
Creating worlds inside our brain.

We watch, we hear, we overstore,
What others say, what others bore.
They never mean the harm we find,
But we grind it down inside our mind.

Mix the words, the acts, the looks,
Collapsing thoughts in tangled hooks.
Serve this curry to ourselves,
Then share the taste with someone else.

The present flees; we chase the past,
Complications growing fast.
Why does the wind throw dust my way?
Why does right still feel astray?

Our minds, a swirl of shadowed hues,
The black it yields, a heavy bruise.
Daydreams twist, but nights won't heal,
Fear is all we seem to feel.

In daylight hours, our hearts despair,
At night, the dreams become a snare.
Overthinking binds our will,
A restless mind, a soul made still.

Dings R Veds…

21. Why Can't I Be Me?

No more ways to tear me down,
A broken heart won't break again.
Comparison fades my light away,
A hero and villain—they're not the same.

I've always been compared to her,
My sister, perfect, they infer.
"She plays well, why can't you?
She draws well, why can't you?"

"She understands, why can't you see?
She's clear in thought, why can't you be?
She's got goals, why can't you try?
She's aggressive, why can't you fly?"

But let me ask, what about me?
I write with heart; why can't she?
I build my world with creativity,
Why can't she dream like me?

I control emotions silently,
Why can't she find that key?
I see how people's minds unfold,
Why can't she understand like me?

I search for truths, big and small,
Why can't she see it all?
We're born to plant our own seed,
Not borrow dreams we do not need.

Maybe this is why I overthink,
Why my self-worth feels on the brink.
But in my pain, I start to see—
There's nothing wrong with just being me.

Dings R Veds…

22. A Heart that Won't Give Up

The Innocent Heart

You hurt me more than words can say,
A storm brews within me every day.
When you draw near to others, leave me behind,
It shatters the peace I hoped to find.

My words, you toss like leaves in the air,
Because I'm a girl, does that mean you don't
care?
If I dared to act the way you do,
Wouldn't your heart feel the breaking too?

A bracelet not mine, but given by another,
I ask you to remove it—it feels like a bother.
Yet if you asked the same of me,
Would I stand as strong, or let it be?

I have no pride, no ego to defend,
Only a pain that refuses to mend.
Your words cut deep, sharp as a knife,
Yet still, I try to rebuild this life.

Not with bandages or fleeting glue,
But with a heart that beats only for you.
An innocent heart, though battered and torn,
Fixes itself, though weary and worn.

For love, it rises, again and again,
Even as it drowns in sorrow's rain.
I carry this ache, this silent scream,
Because you are my hope, my endless dream.

Dings R Veds…

23. She is Me

I saw a girl who reflected as me,
Drowned in a hell no one can see.
She is my mirror, my inner cry,
A child hurt, asking why.

Her burden is mine, though stories divide,
The pain we carry stays locked inside.
Every girl knows this prison's name,
A physical arrestment wrapped in shame.

Why does the world point at us,
Not at the one who broke our trust?
The one who touched without consent,
Without shame, without regret.

Am I wrong—did I allow?
Do you think I wanted it somehow?
No! We're stuck, we freeze, we fight,
But our minds shut down in the night.

It feels like drowning in endless fear,
A silent scream no one will hear.
Our bodies tremble, our voices fade,
Our souls feel crushed, our hearts betrayed.

It feels like fire burning the skin,
A battle we lose before it begins.
We carry the shame, though it isn't ours,
Their crime, their guilt, their scarred hours.

And then we hate what we have to be,
Ashamed of the girl they took from me.
But we didn't allow, we didn't choose,
It's not our fault—it's theirs to lose.

So why does blame fall on the queen,
When the monster's hands remain unseen?
It's time to rise, to shift the weight,
To fight their power, to rewrite fate.

No girl should drown in this silent pain,
Her crown intact, she'll stand again.

Dings R Veds…

24. She Doesn't Allow...

I saw a girl today, and she looked like me.
Not someone else—she is me.
My inner girl, trapped in pain,
Still living through that storm again.

She carries wounds from years before,
A child's heart broken, shaken to the core.
She faced things no child should,
Things no one ever understood.

The world around her turned away,
While her innocence was torn that day.
She didn't ask, she didn't allow,
But they blamed her somehow.

Her mind froze, her body still,
Fighting against someone's will.
It wasn't her fault, but shame grew deep,
A secret burden she'd always keep.

It feels like fire, it feels like stone,
A little girl left all alone.
And now, as I look, I see her there,
My younger self, hurt and scared.

But she is me, and I am her,
Through the pain, we still endure.
Though the world may never see,
That little girl still lives in me.

Dings R Veds…

25. Can I Move on From You?

He waits to hear my voice tonight,
Hoping I'll speak, make things right.
But don't expect "I love you" here,
Those words I longed for, year by year.

Dreams we held can break and fade,
Promises lost, choices made.
I thought you'd want my heart to stay,
But you just need me to walk away.

Not "I miss you" or "I'll try again,"
But words that free us from this pain:
"Can I move on from you at last?"
The future waits, leave the past.

So here I stand, my heart unsure,
Speaking what's real, nothing more.
A simple truth, a quiet plea:
"Can I move on, and just be me?

Dings R Veds…

26. He Doesn't Want My Heart to Stay

I thought he waited for my voice,
Hoped for love, a heartfelt choice.
But now I see, I was so wrong,
His silence had been cold all along.

I thought he longed to hear "I love you,"
But that was never what he knew.
The words he's waiting for, so clear,
Are the ones I dreaded, full of fear.

He doesn't want my heart to stay,
He wants me to be the one to say:
"Can I move on? Is this the end?"
To give him freedom, not to mend.

I held on tight, I hoped for more,
But he's already closed the door.
The love I thought was burning true
Was only a shadow—I never knew.

Dings R Veds…

27. Raising Above the Ashes

I had a love, but it wasn't pure.

It was just a fleeting change we feel in our teens.

I fell in love with you—not because you were

warm when I held you, but because you made my heart skip a beat whenever I looked at you.

You gave me an unfinished love, a love that was

never meant to last.

You missed what it means to truly care. Instead,

you chased your own goals—not for love, but for

lust.

You played your part well, using me for your desires.

And I, innocent and trusting, gave you everything.

Everyone around me saw it clearly. They blamed You.

"You're not perfect," they said. "You're not worthy of true love."

They told me I was being exploited, but I didn't

believe them.

Not until you left me alone in the dark, where every path seemed to lead nowhere.

That's when it hit me—oh my God, He used me.
I was nothing but a pillow for you, a way to satisfy
your lust, to boost your ego, to feel powerful.
You never cared for my love.
You never valued my care, my efforts, my
protectiveness, or the purity of my feelings.

Now I see you for what you are.
You were the worst kind of lesson, but a lesson, nonetheless.
You taught me how to recognize and handle people like you—those who play games with emotions.

You'll never see the same version of me again.
The person you knew is gone.
I've learned, I've grown, and I'll rise above the
darkness you left me in.

Dings R Veds…

28. The Swoop in Your Eyes

Whenever I see your eyes, I feel weak.
That's why I avoid looking at you.
But you make it easier to let go when you choose other girls over me and ignore me.
You've turned my admiration into pain, fueling my self-worth to rise from the hurt.
I'm struggling without you, but I know one day, I'll move on and find peace.

Dings R Veds…

29. Dark Whisper

You walked into my life,
Like a whisper in the dark,
A light I held so close,
A fire that warmed my heart.

I gave you everything,
My dreams, my soul, my trust.
But you chose another,
And left me in the dust.

Every moment now is heavy,
Your face, your laugh, your name.
It haunts me like a shadow,
An endless, aching flame.

You loved her, my friend,
And tore my world apart.
How cruel of you to steal,
The pieces of my heart.

I cry when no one sees,
The nights are long and cold.
Your memory clings to me,
A story left untold.

Why did you come to break me,
To leave me this way?
I carry the weight of you,
Each and every day.

I'm trying to move, I swear,
But the pain won't let me be.
You're gone, but you're here,
Still stealing pieces of me.

Dings R Veds…

30. The Same Moon

There's a difference in how you see the moon.
When you stare at it from a corner,
Trapped behind walls and hidden by the cage,
It's still the same moon,
But the feeling is distant, cold,
Almost unreachable.

Then, when you're released,
When the cage no longer holds you,
When no more bricks can break you,
You look up again,
And the moon feels different.
It's the same moon,
But the freedom gives it a new light,
A warmth you never knew before.

The same moon,
But it feels like it's finally yours.

Dings R Veds…

31. The Cycle of Trends

One day,
A new trend will become an old reel.
What once was fresh,
Vibrant, and full of life,
Will fade into the backdrop,
Forgotten like yesterday's news.

The things we chase today,
The moments we capture and share,
Will lose their shine,
Replaced by something newer,
Faster, more exciting.

But in the quiet corners,
Those old reels will live,
Reminders of who we were,
What we loved,
And how quickly the world moves on.

One day,
The new will be old,
And we'll look back,
Wondering why we ever let it go.

Dings R Veds…

32. The Unseen Battle

Never judge an over thinker.
They fight with monsters you can't imagine,
Not the ones from stories or pictures.
These monsters are shapeless,
With long, grasping hands and endless legs,
Drenched in the dark of Vantablack.

They scratch and tear,
Leaving wounds that never heal,
Draining every ounce of life,
Using blood as their fuel.
They break in without warning,
Whispering fears that never stop.

You see the scars on our bodies
And call us foolish,
As if we're weak or lost.
But these scars are proof
Of battles fought in silence,
Against monsters that never rest.

This fight is endless, unseen,
Yet it consumes everything.
Don't dismiss the pain—
We're not fighting for peace,
We're fighting just to stay alive.

Dings R Veds…

33. The Confort of the Darkness

I was forced to stay in a dark room,
Scared of the corners, haunted by nightmares.
I escaped, chasing a light that seemed far,
A door that promised something better.
I opened it and fell into a world of people.

At first, it felt like a relief,
A soft, cool bear in my hands,
Kind faces, warm gestures.
But then, things shifted,
The masks began to fade,
Their words turned sharp,
Melting into something I couldn't trust.

I realized the dark, with its screaming monsters,
Felt safer than the light of their fading faces,
Their words cutting deeper than any shadow,
It made me long for the silence of that dark room,
Where at least the fear was honest.

Dings R Veds…

34. Cold Days

Days and nights keep passing by,
But my heart, it doesn't sleep, doesn't eat,
It just wants to drown in the imaginary world
Where you and I were once complete.

Dings R Veds…

35. The Power of Being

The power of being you and me
Will be the same,
But being you is different,
And being me is different.
You and me admire different,
Yet together, we create something unique.

Dings R Veds…

36. Behind the stained glass

My life is stuck,
Everything seemed beautiful once,
But now, what happened?
The way I was treated,
The way I was judged,
The way I was used…
It all paints me as a bad girl,
Lost, unsure of my path.

I'm cheating myself,
Trying to prove I'm good,
Scrubbing the dirt off my glass,
But the stain never fades.
I'm not ready to change the glass,
Even though it's ready to shine.

Afraid of changes,
I hide behind walls
That lead to darker paths.
I know them well,
Yet I linger,

Unready to move
To the next pillar,
To the light beyond.

Dings R Veds…

37. Misnaned Beauty

They see the hibiscus,
and call it a cactus,
Their gossip sharp,
turning beauty to thorn.

But the flower stands,
unchanged,
Knowing it's still
a hibiscus at heart.

Dings R Veds…

38. A Flash of Menories

Whenever your memories strike,
They flash through my mind,
Shattering the peace,
Of my once carefree, childlike time.

The songs that once gave me vibes,
Now sound like the ugliest chimes.
The ground where we played,
The snaps we saved,
The gifts we exchanged,
All now seem like a charade.

Leave all that behind,
Let it fade into a dream.
One second, take a breath,
Close your eyes, and see,
Our memories, the flashbacks in mind.

And now, tell me,
What did I ever do for you?
Why did you cheat,
And tear my heart in two?

This will be my last word,
My last moment of thought,
For you and all we had.
Here is the letter from my heart,
Torn to pieces, shattered apart.

Thank you for everything,
For the long time we shared,
Destroyed in a single minute,
By the betrayal you declared.

Dings R Veds…

39.Letter to My X

Hey, my dear ex-friend,

How's life treating you?

I imagine you're doing well,

Spreading your happiness like a ripple in water.

I need to share something,

That gift you gave,

A small mirror,

It talks to me now.

It shows me who I was,

The villain in your story,

Your reflection,

Was just a mask you crafted.

Now I see a stronger girl,

Forged from your lies,

You taught her so much,

Without saying a word.

You taught her not to fall too hard,
Not to spill her secrets,
Not to rely on anyone,
To stand on her own.

You revealed the world's betrayal,
Its cruel games,
But you didn't leave me in the dark,
You led me to the light.

You didn't shatter my peace,
You helped me see through the acts,
Helped me open my eyes,
For that, I thank you.

Dings R Veds…

40. The Shattered Diamond

A diamond, beautiful and worth infinity with careful hands,
Gleaming only when clear, crushed to dust by a heavy rock,
Now flying unseen, its brilliance lost,
As people only see the rock's strength,
Forgetting the diamond's shattered,
irreplaceable value,
Leaving the rock to mock the fragility
Of what was once eternal,
What once lit the dark with its unique fire,
Now scattered, invisible, forgotten,
While the rock stands solid,
Its weight admired,
Its power feared,
And the diamond's silent remnants
Become the sorrowful whispers of what
could have been,
Forever lost in the shadows of an unyielding
world.

Dings R Veds…

41. Finding Confort in Pain

When life flows smooth, everything feels

great,

But when darkness falls, hope fades away.

Still, we search for something better,

Not the same old drama,

Not the same familiar light.

In the difference,

We find a strange comfort,

Even within the pain.

Dings R Veds…

42. The Same, Yet Not

chilling in my vibe,
the same old table sits sturdy,
a witness to my quiet rebellions,
a new refill pen rests between fingers,
the same book lies open,
its pages replaced,
but the story continues to spill,
raw, unfiltered,
like thoughts I cannot cage.

the yellow wall holds my gaze,
once blank, now littered
with words I didn't plan to write,
phrases born of restless nights,
a canvas for the mind
that refuses to be still.

I build this space around me,
piece by piece,
like the architecture of my thoughts—
messy, unfinished,
but mine,
always mine.

each day comes dressed the same,

yet nothing stays,

everything shifts,

and it is not the day

but the way I see it

that tells me who I am.

Dings R Veds…

43. Broken Before

You thought your actions broke me,
But I was already broken.
Your words hit first,
Straight to my heart,
Leaving nothing behind.

It wasn't what you did,
But what you said,
And the quiet after,
That ended me long ago.

Dings R Veds…

44. The Choice in Your Hands

Life hands you both—
A flower, soft and tender,
And a thorn, sharp and cruel.
It's in your hands,
What you choose to hold.

Will you cradle the petals,
Their fragrance, their warmth?
Or let the thorn
Pierce your skin,
And stain your grip with pain?

Both come together,
You cannot escape,
But the choice is yours
To keep the beauty
And let the pain fall away.

Dings R Veds…

45. The Endless Loop

An overthinker sits in silence, Their mind a restless sea.
Every thought turns to "what if,"
And every "what if" turns to doubt.

Decisions slip through their fingers,
Lost in the waves of maybe.
The paths ahead blur together,
None feeling right, none feeling wrong.

They circle back to the start,
Trapped in a loop they can't escape.
The answers hide in the stillness,
But stillness is the hardest place to be.

Dings R Veds…

46. Freedom We Seek

We need freedom,
Not for long phone calls,
But just to write our thoughts
In a diary,
Keeping them close,
Hidden from the world.

We need freedom,
Not for closing the door,
Hiding behind a screen,
But to lock it tight
And cry in silence,
Without the world hearing.

We need freedom,
Not for outings or parties,
But to stay in the spaces
Where we feel safe,
Where the noise can't reach,
Where we can breathe.

We need freedom,
Not to escape the world,
But to find peace within it.
To feel the warmth of the sun
Without the weight of expectations,
To speak without fear of judgment,
To love without losing ourselves.

But what if that freedom;
Is always just out of reach?
What if the door stays closed,
The diary remains locked,
The heart left to shout in silence,
Waiting for a freedom
We may never find?

And in the end,
This is what we call freedom:
A quiet longing
That never truly fades.

Dings R Veds…

47. A New Beginning

Sorry… I can't fix what's broken,
But maybe sorry, mixed with effort and change,
Can rebuild what was lost.

It won't be the same,
But new can come from the old,
A chance to start fresh,
To heal in ways we never imagined.
Sometimes, the broken parts
Create space for something better,
Something that wasn't possible
Until the cracks Sometimes

Dings R Veds…

48. To My Magical Pillow

You hold my tears but never got wet;
You saved my secrets but never said.
You carried my pain but never got worried;
You stayed firm from my hard punches but never tried to give back,

You carried all my feelings but never filled off;
They separate you in people but not in my heart,
You change my panic into grin when i clasp you;
Your structure may differ but not your bear...

When they left me alone, only you stayed, no ego to show...!
Thanks for everything.

Dings R Veds...

49. You and Me

We meet,

No contact!

We speak,

No romance!

We respect,

No respond!

Yeah! It's more paining than long distance,

Want to fall in your chest,

But can't even look at your gaze.

Let me grab your arm,

So that I can feel my storm.

Let me open up my heart,

So that you can fix my part

Nothing is in our gaze,

Everything is our fate,

Be aware I'm there for you,

To make your dream come true...

Dings R Veds…

50. Don't Trust Them...

Don't trust their words,
Trust their action.
Don't trust their promise,
Trust their efforts.

Don't trust their lip.
Trust their eye.
Don't trust their face,
Trust their heart.

Don't trust them,
Trust you, the way you look at them,
Not the way they make you to look.

Dings R Veds...

The Ending Note...

The voice around me...

If they are not right here with me,
I want be right there at in my future.
If their words aren't aiming my heart,
I won't hold my aim tightly than before.

They pulled me down, if they didn't,
I won't see my new world.
If they didn't underestimate me,
I will be the same girl who doesn't know her talent.

The road blokes which i met it is not road blocks,
It is my goal box which hold many experiences to guide me in future.
For every problem I have solution within me,
Why should I have to search it out of my world.

You are not one you are many...

Dings R Veds...

If I can then you can...

Notable quotes from people I've met along the way:

Born to Fly

Dream high, beyond the sky,
No matter wings are small,
Keep vision bright and just dare to learn.
You are born to fly.

BUMIKA [air hostess]
indigo flight @10.10.2024

"Dream Bold, Live Bright"

"Be yourself, do what feels right,
Live in the moment, shine your light.

If you dare to dream, don't let it slip,
Have the courage to make it a lifelong trip."

Ridu Varshini Ramasamy

(My Bossy Sister)

If You Can Then I Can...

I always believe when someone can
Do it i can do it , when i can do
It ,anybody can do it
People say do or die ,but i believe
Do it before you die

- Thulasimathi Murugesan...
(She made history as the first Indian woman shuttler to win a Paralympic silver medal)

Oh Look

Look at what I have become

You hurt me despite my scars,

You saw me bleed,

And ignored me pleas,

I trusted you,

You left me, when you were what I need,

You saw the blade in the drawer,

And you saw fresh blood stains in the bed sheets,

You heard my screams when I was asleep,

You closed the door,

Because your sleep as disturbed,

You fucking ignored me,

The blades have become a brush,

The blood has become the paint,

I have become a masterpiece,

Of my own pain,

Not even one phone call,

Not even one it's okay,

Not even one how are you today,

When you talk to me sometimes, you say

your words are as pure as the saints,

Now! There is Not even a soul who would

accept me for me!

Good night, it's time for sleep..

-tsk

-Teja Sivakumar

A Girl Who Mirror My Soul..

Life's Purposeful Turns

I strongly believe that all things align,

Every moment, every sign.

Even the hardships, the moments that sting,

Happen for reasons the future will bring.

Though some may hurt and feel unkind,

They shape our souls, they clear our minds.

In every trial, in every fall, There's a purpose behind it all.

-Ark

A R Kaviya

My Cousin With Crime..

Closing Words

As I reach the end of this book, I want to express my heartfelt gratitude to you—my reader, my fellow dreamer, my silent companion in these words.

This book is not just a collection of poetry; it is a reflection of emotions that often go unheard. If even a single verse resonated with you, made you feel understood, or gave you

STRENGTH, THEN THIS JOURNEY HAS BEENWORTH IT.

I would love to hear your thoughts, feelings, and reflections. Your feedback means the world to me, and I welcome you to connect with me. You can reach me at Dingsrveds19@gmail.com —whether to share your thoughts, your own stories, or simply to say hello.

Thank you for being part of this journey. May your voice always find its way to the world, and may your heart never feel alone.

With love and gratitude,

Dings R Veds (Vedha Varna R)

The Beginning

And finally it's me…

"May these words be the voice you needed, the comfort you sought, and the strength you never knew you had."

Vedha Varna Ramasamy…

(Dings R Veds) Dingsrveds19@gmail.com